CREATING HIGH-IMPACT TRAINING

A Practical Guide To Successful Training Outcomes

Richard Y. Chang

Richard Chang Associates, Inc.
Publications Division
Irvine, California

CREATING HIGH-IMPACT TRAINING

A Practical Guide To Successful Training Outcomes

Richard Y. Chang

Library of Congress Catalog Card Number
94-68229

ISBN 1-883553-41-5

Third printing March 1998

Company names used in this book are purely hypothetical and are not intented to suggest or depict actual company names.

Richard Chang Associates, Inc.
Publications Division
15265 Alton Parkway, Suite 300
Irvine, CA 92618
(800) 756-8096 • Fax (714) 727-7007
www.richardchangassociates.com

ACKNOWLEDGMENTS

About The Author

Richard Y. Chang is President and CEO of Richard Chang Associates, Inc., a diversified organizational improvement consulting firm based in Irvine, California. He is internationally recognized for his management strategy, quality improvement, organization development, customer satisfaction, and human resource development expertise.

The author would like to acknowledge the support of the entire team of professionals at Richard Chang Associates, Inc. for their contribution to the guidebook development process. In addition, special thanks are extended to the many client organizations who have helped to shape the practical ideas and proven methods shared in this guidebook.

Additional Credits

Editor/Reviewer: Ruth Stingley

Graphic Layout: Suzanne Jamieson

Cover Design: John Odam Design Associates

PREFACE

The 1990's have already presented individuals and organizations with some very difficult challenges to face and overcome. So who will have the advantage as we move toward the year 2000 and beyond?

The advantage will belong to those with a commitment to continuous learning. Whether on an individual basis or as an entire organization, one key ingredient to building a continuous learning environment is *The Practical Guidebook Collection* brought to you by the Publications Division of Richard Chang Associates, Inc.

After understanding the future *"learning needs"* expressed by our clients and other potential customers, we are pleased to publish *The Practical Guidebook Collection*. These guidebooks are designed to provide you with proven, *"real-world"* tips, tools, and techniques—on a wide range of subjects—that you can apply in the workplace and/or on a personal level immediately.

Once you've had a chance to benefit from *The Practical Guidebook Collection*, please share your feedback with us. We've included a brief *Evaluation and Feedback Form* at the end of the guidebook that you can fax to us at (714) 756-0853.

With your feedback, we can continuously improve the resources we are providing through the Publications Division of Richard Chang Associates, Inc.

Wishing you successful reading,

Richard Y. Chang
President and CEO
Richard Chang Associates, Inc.

TABLE OF CONTENTS

"Anyone who stops learning is old, whether at twenty or eighty. Anyone who keeps learning stays young."

Henry Ford

"It is what we think we know already that often prevents us from learning."

Claude Bernard

CHAPTER ONE

INTRODUCTION

"The trouble with our age is all signposts and no destination."

-Louis Kronenberger

Why Read This Guidebook?

Training will never become obsolete. As long as technology changes, new people enter the work force, and businesses strive to improve, organizations will need training. The term *"training"* may change (*e.g., it's currently referred to as learning, coaching, facilitating, etc.*), but the concept remains the same: people continually need help in mastering new skills, applying new knowledge, and/or adjusting their attitudes.

What many people fail to realize is that training is itself a skill that needs to be learned. Expert trainers know the hours involved in learning how to train. Novice trainers soon realize that training isn't an easy endeavor. And non-trainers often don't know where to begin.

Consider LeAnn, a new trainer . . .

at a computer superstore. The cashiers aren't using a new check procedure they were trained to use. Upper management has asked LeAnn  to re-train them, but she thinks the cashiers know the procedure but aren't using it for other reasons. She feels additional training won't help. What should she do?

Or what about Eduardo, a line manager . . .

at a rubber manufacturing plant? The vice president targeted Eduardo to train the employees in his department to use new rubber molds the  company purchased. He did. Three months later, Eduardo notices that the employees are rarely using the new molds. Where did he go wrong?

These examples illustrate the point that while training is a common occurrence, it doesn't always solve problems or improve performance. Why? Because not all training is high-impact training. Something went awry in the training processes at both the computer superstore and the rubber manufacturing plant. Some training makes no impact at all on an organization; other training makes a dent. Only high-impact training has lasting results.

This guidebook looks at the whole picture of training. Where do you start? How do you begin? Who's your audience? What's involved in producing learning tools? How do you deliver training successfully? Why does training continue after the program is finished? And more.

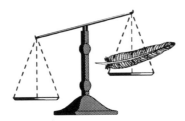

No-Impact Training

Low-Impact Training

High-Impact Training

As a greater number of organizations are looking for ways to cut costs, training is being scrutinized. In some cases, this means that training departments *(or others conducting training)* have to prove the value of their training efforts. *Creating High-Impact Training* addresses that issue. In other cases, it means that non-trainers are being thrust into the arena of training and don't know what to do. *Creating High-Impact Training* provides a clear look at the complete training process, from start to finish. It will guide those who desire to train successfully.

Who Should Read This Guidebook?

Creating High-Impact Training provides new trainers like LeAnn with an approach to training that covers their questions. By applying the first phase of the High-IMPACT Training™ Model presented in this guidebook, LeAnn will learn that identifying training needs is a critical step in the training process. By analyzing her potential training situation, she might prove her hunch that training is unnecessary and provide herself with other solutions for upper management.

Individuals and managers given a training assignment will find this guidebook indispensable. It's a must-read for the uninitiated. Like Eduardo, they might not know how to make training a successful venture. This guidebook is a non-trainer's road map to effective training.

And finally, even seasoned, professional trainers will uncover valuable information in this guidebook. *Creating High-Impact Training* goes beyond traditional training processes. If you can plan and implement a successful training program, but you're not sure how to link training to organizational impact or how to make those training results last, read on.

It doesn't matter whether you're a manager, a novice trainer, a professional trainer, or an individual faced with helping others learn. If you want your training to have a great impact on your organization, if you want job performance to increase, if you desire your training to be successful, read *Creating High-Impact Training*.

When And How To Use It

Your best bet is to use the model presented in this guidebook before training starts, because careful planning increases your success rate. In the planning stage you might even concur, like LeAnn, that training won't solve the problem. Either way, you'll save yourself time, money, and major headaches.

If you're thrown into a training situation, at whatever point, *Creating High-Impact Training* will help you aim your training or even turn it around so that it's headed in the right direction.

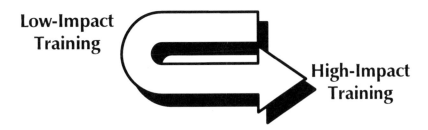

Low-Impact Training

High-Impact Training

If you're new to training, you'll want to read the whole guidebook to acquaint yourself with the steps involved in the High-IMPACT Training Model. It covers all the bases.

If you already know the fundamentals of training, you might not need to read every chapter in great detail. Skim through those you're familiar with, and concentrate on those new to you. Each of the phases covered in this guidebook are covered more fully in separate guidebooks. For example, if you're interested in making training results last, you might want to check out the companion guidebook devoted fully to that phase—*Make Your Training Results Last*.

Creating High-Impact Training is meant to take the *"what ifs,"* the fears, and the negative feelings out of the training process, and replace them with an approach you can use confidently. Training can be a great opportunity if you know how to go about it successfully!

HIGH-IMPACT TRAINING

Training is often treated as a quick fix. Do your customer service representatives need to improve their phone skills? Send them to a seminar. Is your sales force behind in their yearly quotas? Have the training department run a motivational video.

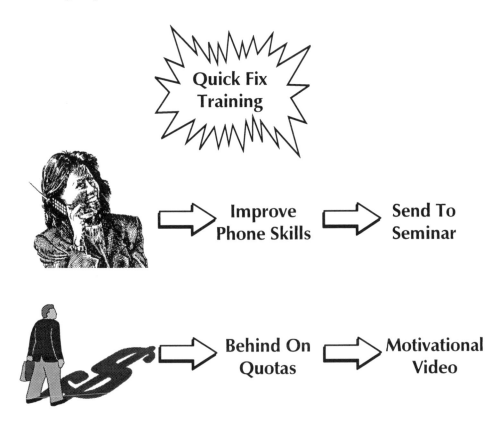

And if the phone skills and quotas improve right after training occurs, upper management is satisfied. At least until six months down the line when it's clear that the training had little long-term impact.

If training is to be more than a Band-Aid that works itself loose over time, you need to have a plan. Training that actually improves job performance, that contributes to an organization's bottom line, isn't a haphazard affair that can be assigned to any individual. It's a process that must be followed carefully if it's meant to have impact.

Training Myths

Think about the following myths commonly associated with training.

Training Myths

Myth #1 → Training is a single event.

Myth #2 → Training is a classroom experience.

Myth #3 → Great program materials ensure successful training.

Myth #4 → An effective trainer produces effective training.

Myth #5 → Once you've evaluated a program, training ends.

Have you heard any of these before? Maybe no one has articulated them to you, but such perceptions thrive in organizations today. Let's look at each of the myths separately.

The Myths Exposed

Myth #1: Training is a single event.

Training doesn't occur only on the day it's scheduled. It requires careful planning before it's implemented, and post-training measurement and follow-through. Most people might agree that learning tools need to be produced, but how many realize that successful trainers spend countless hours before they even think about composing worksheets, choosing videos, or preparing overhead transparencies? And the hours spent measuring the results and tracking the success of training often translate into additional days of work.

Myth #2: Training is a classroom experience.

For some, training is a classroom experience. But for countless others, training occurs on-the-job. In fact, on-the-job training accounts for the large majority of training situations. Traditional classroom training is on the decline and moving toward a *"just-in-time"* form of training in work groups and project teams on the job. Successful trainers fit the training approach to their particular group of trainees.

Myth #3: Great program materials ensure successful training.

You can have the greatest program materials in the world, but if you don't know how to use them effectively or your presentation falls flat because your delivery was poor, it's doubtful your participants will consider the training a success. Program materials can contribute to successful training, but their contribution is only one piece of the puzzle.

Myth #4: An effective trainer produces effective training.

This myth is closely tied to the previous one. An effective trainer is essential to successful training; but, again, his or her contribution is limited. What if a marvelous trainer is using outdated material? Is that effective training? Or what if that same trainer is teaching a skill that's too technical for the trainees? Or suppose the trainees already know what they're being taught? Does successful training depend only upon the skill of the trainer? Clearly, no.

| Training | Evaluation | On-the-Job Skills |

Myth #5: Once you've evaluated a program, training ends.

If you're not a professional trainer, you'll likely assume this is correct. But wait: should you gauge the success of training solely on whether the participants enjoyed the program and felt they learned from it and could apply the learning back on the job? Training goes far beyond this point.

You have to assess whether the training participants have applied their new skills on the job. You need to analyze whether the training has affected the organization in a positive manner. And finally, you have to follow-through. Unless new skills are maintained, you'll be in Eduardo's position—three months down the line, his employees weren't using the new molds he had trained them to use. Successful training is still in operation months after the training sessions end.

Doing It Right

Training can be much more than a quick fix. If handled correctly, it becomes a remedy that successfully improves job performance. Training that works involves fleshing out your training needs, deciding upon the right approach to take, choosing the correct learning tools, applying training techniques, measuring the results, and following-through to ensure lasting impact.

Doctors use a similar method. Let's say your hand is red and swollen. The doctor must first determine the problem. Did you

catch your hand in the car door or is the cause a splinter or perhaps even a bacterial infection? Your doctor can then decide upon her approach (*e.g., remove splinter, apply ice, prescribe antibiotics, etc.*) and assess what tools she needs.

Suppose a splinter is the problem. The doctor implements her plan, using tweezers to remove the splinter, then applies antiseptic ointment and a bandage. She hands you a prescription for

more ointment, and asks you to return in a week for a check-up. You notice a decrease in pain and swelling. At the follow-up visit, all redness and swelling are gone.

If the doctor had eliminated any of these steps, your problem could have been misdiagnosed or incorrectly treated or caused you additional pain. It's critical that she did it right, and it's critical that you approach your training in the same manner. You have to do it right if you want great results. Follow the High-IMPACT Training™ Model that's presented in the next chapter, and prepare for training that works. The health of your organization is at risk!

CHAPTER TWO WORKSHEET: GETTING PAST THE MYTHS

Consider the training that takes place in your organization. Would you say that the myths presented in this chapter indicate what your organization thinks about training? Look at each myth separately and check whether those in your organization agree or disagree with it.

1. Training is a single event.

Agree? ☐   Disagree? ☐

2. Training is a classroom experience.

Agree? ☐   Disagree? ☐

3. Great program materials ensure successful training.

Agree? ☐   Disagree? ☐

4. An effective trainer produces effective training.

Agree? ☐   Disagree? ☐

5. Once you've evaluated a program, training ends?

Agree? ☐   Disagree? ☐

6. For each myth that you checked *"Agree,"* write a brief response challenging that myth.

_____

_____

_____

_____

_____

_____

_____

_____

_____

_____

_____

_____

_____

_____

_____

_____

A MODEL FOR SUCCESS

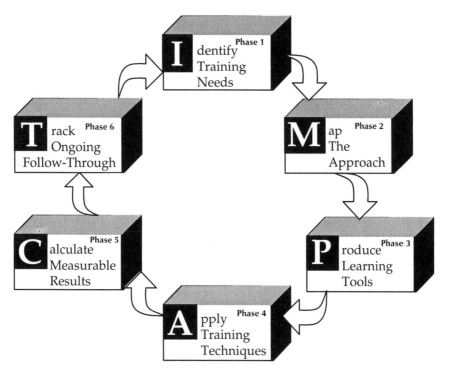

The High-IMPACT Training™ Model

In training, there's much at stake. For example, suppose your training situation involves one-on-one teaching of a new employee, Ralph, for a period of two days. You're investing your time and his time *(a total of 4 days).* If you succeed in your effort? The return on your investment will be good. If you handle it poorly? Much more than four days of work will be lost.

When a training effort involves hundreds or thousands of people across the country, the stakes become tremendously high. In that situation, you certainly wouldn't leave training to chance.

But even if your training effort falls closer to the first example, you should plan your training carefully, implement it strategically, and follow-through. And if you use the High-IMPACT Training™ Model, you'll increase your odds substantially.

The High-IMPACT Training Model

It's referred to as the High-IMPACT Training Model, not only because following it will have tremendous impact on your organization, but also because IMPACT is an acronym for the six phases of the model.

The High-IMPACT Training Model focuses on the importance of effective, targeted training. The table below illustrates what occurs during each of its six phases.

PHASE	DESCRIPTION
1. **I** dentify Training Needs	Determine if and how training can play a role in improving job performance; target training outcomes.
2. **M** ap The Approach	Choose the appropriate training approach(es) that will best support the targeted outcomes and improve job performance.
3. **P** roduce Learning Tools	Produce all training/coaching components (*e.g., materials, audiovisual aids, job aids, etc.*).
4. **A** pply Training Techniques	Deliver the training as designed to ensure successful results.
5. **C** alculate Measurable Results	Assess whether your training/coaching accomplished actual performance improvement, communicate the results, and redesign the process as necessary.
6. **T** rack Ongoing Follow-Through	Hone in on the techniques that individuals and organizations can use to ensure that the impact of their training does not diminish.

How Is It Different?

The High-IMPACT Training Model is a practical approach to training. And it continues where most training models leave off—at the evaluation stage. The High-IMPACT Training Model doesn't stop abruptly after participants rank the trainer and the training program. It gears up at this phase in an effort to prove its value to the organization and to maintain training results.

Training Evaluation

Maintaining Training Results

Trainers who stop at program evaluation are defeating their purpose. How can you truly assess your training effort's value without documenting how well the participants have transferred their learning into on-the-job action? You can't. You have to calculate measurable results to show the link between training and organizational impact.

And long after the video you showed during training is forgotten, you still need results. How do you keep the learning intact and job performance increasing? Check out the last phase in the High-IMPACT Training Model—*Track Ongoing Follow-Through*. It will give you the follow-through tips missing from other training models.

Let's step in as one organization sees the need for training.

George Chiroma, the head of the Housekeeping Department . . .

at the Smithton Hotel, was facing a dilemma. Lately, the customer comment cards reflected concern regarding the cleanliness of the rooms. Upper management cornered George and wanted to know why.

Since the problem couldn't be traced to just a few of the housekeeping personnel, George thought that training would help the entire staff of thirty-six individuals. Upper management called in Rachael, one of the corporate training consultants, to lend George a hand. Rachael had a high success rate at other Smithton Hotels in the national chain, and they hoped her expertise would take care of the job performance problem.

Want to see the model in action? Watch as the Housekeeping Department at Smithton Hotel discovers how to create high-impact training.

CHAPTER THREE WORKSHEET:
IS YOUR TRAINING HIGH-IMPACT?

1. Briefly describe your organization's approach to training.

_____

_____

2. What are the strengths of this approach?

_____

_____

3. What are the weaknesses?

_____

_____

4. Compare your company's approach to the phases in the High-IMPACT Training Model.

_____

_____

_____

_____

IDENTIFYING TARGETED TRAINING NEEDS

Many organizations and trainers alike fail to identify their targeted training needs. Why? They're sure that training is necessary, and they think that they already know what should be included in their training program. In some cases training may be obvious, but in other cases you'll need to search further for the cause of your situation.

All training efforts require a needs analysis. You may be eager to travel the training route, but you'd better first make sure that the trip will be worthwhile.

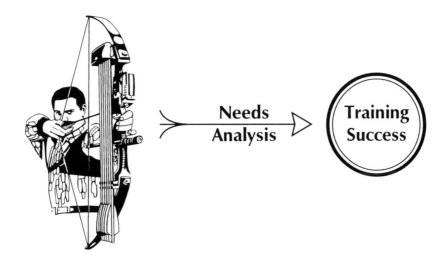

Identifying targeted training needs is the first step on the path to effective training. In this phase of the High-IMPACT Training Model, you'll undertake a needs analysis to ensure that the training you do addresses your particular situation. When you do a needs analysis, you focus your attention on the target and identify the means for getting there. You also involve others in the process and help them understand the issues you are all facing.

To complete a needs analysis, you can follow six basic steps. They are:

Assessing Your Current Situation

In a needs analysis, assessing your current situation provides a clear definition of the problem. All of your other actions in the needs analysis depend on the accuracy of your assessment. It's a critical first step.

To view the complete picture of your current situation, ask yourself the following three questions:

Where are we now?

Begin your needs analysis by exploring the current situation. Start by noting what you already know about your situation. If you've assembled a team to help you tackle training, ask the others to define the current situation as they see it. Involving others right from the start is a good way to begin establishing a partnership for the whole process.

Why do we think we need training?

The obvious answer to this is, *"We need training to address our situation."* Go beyond the obvious. Ask, *"Why now?"* Think further about the issue. Is there a history for this situation? What is the issue, problem, or situation that is creating the need or demand for this training?

What organizational issues are driving the need for training?

This question compels you to look at the larger picture that should be a part of your overall strategy. If you know what the mission, vision, and business objectives of your organization are, you should be able to determine what is going on in your organization that is driving the need for training.

Rachael, the newly arrived trainer . . .

from corporate, asked George to choose a couple of individuals to help in the training effort. *"Pick people directly involved with housekeeping,"* she suggested. *"Their input will help."* George chose Thea, one of the supervisors, and Miriam, a full-time housekeeper who had been with the hotel a few years.

The team got down to business. The need for training, the group agreed, was fairly obvious. The rooms weren't always properly cleaned *(the current situation)*, mainly due to the high-turnover rate of employees and uncertainty about the cleaning procedures *(the possible causes)*. These factors fueled the need for training. Smithton Hotels wanted the problem taken care of. They were noted for their outstanding service and didn't want a blemish on their record. . . .

Envisioning Your Future

Envisioning your future involves defining and understanding what training will accomplish. When you think about how the future will look if your training efforts are successful, you often discover aspects of your vision that have nothing to do with training but are critical to the success of your efforts. If you uncover these elements early in your needs analysis, you can address them as well.

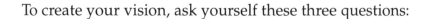
To create your vision, ask yourself these three questions:

1.   Where do we want to be?

Just as you carefully developed a description of your current situation, you must now develop an equally careful description of the future. Use your imagination to see your trainees as they would be if the issues of the current situation were successfully addressed.

Don't worry about how you are going to get to this destination right now. Just imagine where you would like to be.

2.   What would success look like?

What would be different if the issues were resolved successfully? Think about how the solution would help the customer and your entire organization. What benefits would result if your vision of the future came true?

3.   Do we have the whole picture?

Your vision of the future must also consider the needs of others. How will your solution benefit the organization as a whole? How will it benefit the customer?

An excellent way to measure the future is to determine if there are any quantifiable measures or data that would indicate success. If numbers or measures are important to your success, include them in your description of the future.

The training team at Smithton Hotel . . .
saw the increase in clean rooms as benefiting the guests of the hotel, helping lead to repeat business. The team set a goal for customer rating of room cleanliness. Customers currently rated room cleanliness an average of 7.2 on a scale of 10. George and the others wanted to see an average of at least 9 within three months and at least 9.5 within six months.

Enlarging the picture also reveals key players outside your group of trainees whose involvement may be essential to the success of your needs analysis. By identifying others who have a stake in the success of your project, you expand your resources and increase your chances of success.

Gathering Information

The information-gathering step is an opportunity for you to collect raw data from whatever sources you feel would be helpful. The three concerns of gathering information are:

Whom to ask
What to ask
How to ask

Whom to ask

In selecting individuals or groups to provide information, ask yourself these questions:

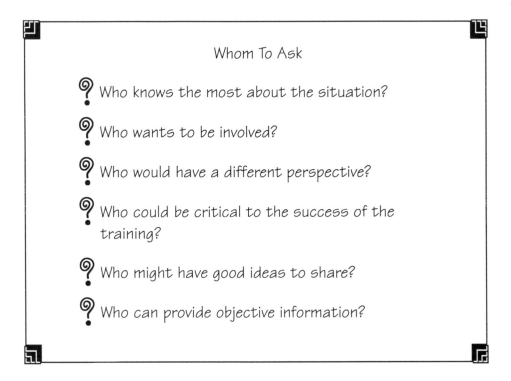

Whom To Ask

- Who knows the most about the situation?

- Who wants to be involved?

- Who would have a different perspective?

- Who could be critical to the success of the training?

- Who might have good ideas to share?

- Who can provide objective information?

Your list of individuals should be representative of those affected by the outcome. Include employees, management, and both internal and external customers.

What to ask

Explain to participants the purpose of the needs analysis and share with them the desired future state. Don't be surprised if they want to add details to the future-state description. You are the best judge of what questions you should ask, but here are a few suggestions:

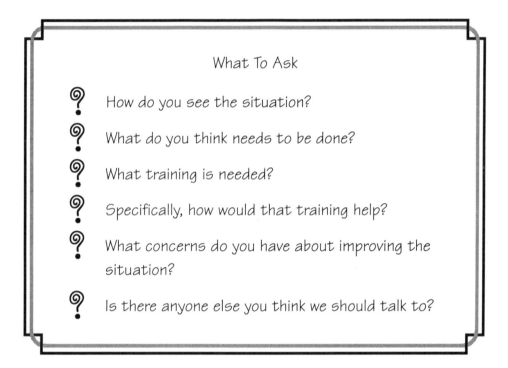

What To Ask

? How do you see the situation?

? What do you think needs to be done?

? What training is needed?

? Specifically, how would that training help?

? What concerns do you have about improving the situation?

? Is there anyone else you think we should talk to?

How to ask

There are endless ways to gather information, but for the purposes of a needs analysis, the most frequently used methods include interviews, focus groups, surveys/questionnaires, document analysis, and observation.

Using a variety of methods is usually best. One example of this would be using interviews with management, surveys and questionnaires with employees, and focus groups with customers—all for the same needs analysis. It really doesn't matter how many methods you employ; concentrate on getting the information you need in a timely and considerate manner.

Sorting Your Information

What should you do with all the information you've gathered? You need to sort it into categories so you can manage it and identify the themes and issues that must be addressed to reach your vision of the future.

When you sort your information into categories, you are looking for consistencies and connections between individual pieces of information. Once you've categorized your information and looked at the significance of each contribution, you can begin to prioritize the issues. How you do this depends on your specific situation.

You might want to start with the category with the most comments, or you might want to start with the positive categories and then list the negative ones. Depending upon your situation, it might be best to address the organizational themes first and then the team themes or individual needs.

Don't lose sight of your objective while you are doing the prioritizing. The importance of the issues should be directly related to achieving your desired future state.

The training team at Smithton Hotel . . .

sifted through the information they had gathered from interviewing the housekeeping personnel and conducting surveys and interviews with customers. *"We've got some good information here,"* Rachael commented. *"You bet,"* George agreed. *"I never would have guessed that hotel guests wanted liquid hand soap instead of wrapped soap bars. But I suppose it would save them time in lathering their hands."* Together the team listed and prioritized the information. . . .

Sharing Your Results

When you share your results with others, your goal is to present the information in a way that will move you forward. Your assessment should be positive and encouraging. Offer hope for solutions to address needs and be prepared with recommendations to share as well.

What to share

Sharing your results with others will be easier if you follow this guide:

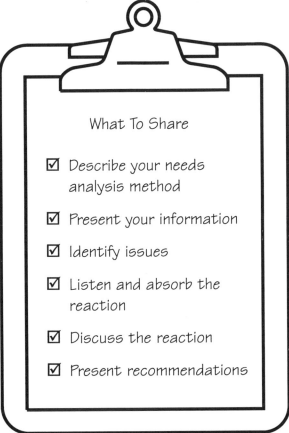

What To Share

☑ Describe your needs analysis method

☑ Present your information

☑ Identify issues

☑ Listen and absorb the reaction

☑ Discuss the reaction

☑ Present recommendations

How to share it

What to share is the challenging part, but how to share it is also an important consideration. Be positive and encouraging. Use every opportunity to draw support and credit the contributions of your trainees.

Consider using visuals or charts to support your information. It gives those present another way to interpret what you're saying. Examples and metaphors can also help your audience understand the material. Be sure to have the raw information available as backup. Someone might ask to see it.

Deciding Your Next Step

The last action in the needs analysis process is to translate the recommendations into a plan of action. To do so, create a list of activities that will be used in the next phases. There are three key elements to a successful action plan:

Determining the actions needed

If your recommendations are not currently worded as actions, rewrite them so they are.

Distributing responsibilities

Each activity in your action plan should be assigned to a specific person. Better yet, ask for volunteers. If a team will be performing the task, record the name of one person on the team as the contact.

Establishing a time line

For each action item, establish a due date for completion of the task. This will give participants a target to aim at and help them focus their activities toward results.

If the information you've gathered and sorted doesn't point toward training, this ends your training process. Your recommendation will be to not pursue training, and your next step will lead you to another endeavor, such as revising a work process.

The training team at Smithton Hotel shared . . .

its results with upper management and the housekeeping personnel. Training was recommended. Later, at a team meeting, Rachael listed the activities the group had yet to complete—coming up with training objectives, designing the approach, etc. *"We'll be doing these as a team,"* she stated. *"Along the way, though, we'll have specific duties."* The group decided that training would start in one month. *"We've got a hectic schedule ahead of us,"* George commented. *"Why don't we get started right away?"* He looked at Rachael. *"What's next?"*

Once you've identified your targeted training needs, you can move confidently to the next phase—mapping the training approach.

CHAPTER FOUR WORKSHEET: TARGETING YOUR NEEDS

1. Briefly describe your current situation.

_____

_____

_____

_____

2. If training is a success, how will your situation change?

_____

_____

_____

_____

3. List the people you need to gather information from. Have you considered:

❏ employees

❏ management

❏ internal customers

❏ external customers

4. With whom will you share your results?

_____

_____

_____

_____

5. What are the recommendations you've come up with as a result of identifying your targeted training needs?

_____

_____

_____

_____

_____

_____

_____

_____

_____

_____

_____

MAPPING THE TRAINING APPROACH

You now know that training is necessary. You've even established what your trainees can do and identified where they need to improve. And you're certain that the improved job performance will pay off for your organization.

But how do you get from point A *(employees in need of training)* to point B *(employees who have improved their on-the-job performance)*?

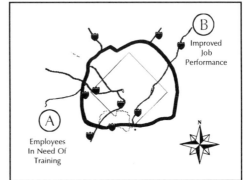

With the actual training, of course. It's the vehicle you'll use to reach your destination. Your job in this phase of the High-IMPACT Training Model is to locate point B and to reserve a sleek, fast-moving car to transport you there. You'll be deciding what you want your trainees to achieve and what is the best approach to help them achieve it.

Mapping the right training approach for your situation requires that you:

> ✍ **Create training objectives**
>
> ✍ **Consider your trainees**
>
> ✍ **Design your approach**

Creating Training Objectives

You know training potentially can take you to the payoff point; you just have to find that point. What are the results you want to achieve? How far will training have to take you? Perhaps you've identified a need for the word processors in your organization to increase the amount of work they handle. They currently type an average of 60 words per minute. The result you want is for them to improve 20 wpm to reach an average of 80 wpm.

In phase one, you gathered baseline measurements and identified that performance gaps exist. Your intent in this first step of phase two is to create actual objectives. You must specifically define what you want training to accomplish; then, you need to create the objectives that will help you reach that goal.

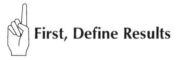 **First, Define Results**    **Then, Create Learning Objectives**

For the word processors, one learning objective that might help them achieve the desired result is learning to use every key on the keyboard. What will it take for your employees to bridge their performance gap? Whatever it will take becomes the learning objectives for your training effort.

Current Performance

Desired Performance

Learning Objectives

Rachael explained to the team . . .

that more planning was ahead. *"Slapping together a training program isn't the answer,"* she said. *"We've got more to do if we want the training to work."*

Together the team worked to identify the results they wanted. *"That's easy,"* Thea spoke up. *"The hotel guests want extra-clean rooms."* *"Isn't that what they've always wanted?"* Rachael asked. Thea nodded. *"Let's look at the results of our surveys and interviews. That information will help us describe an extra-clean room,"* Rachael prodded. *"We need to identify exactly what each person should be doing so that our result is an extra-clean room."*

On a flipchart, the team listed what the hotel guests wanted. An extra-clean room meant thoroughly clean carpets, shiny mirrors with no streaks, scrubbed sinks and tubs, clean towels and washcloths, etc. After the team members exhausted their ideas, Rachael asked, *"What needs to be learned in order to achieve these results? . . .*

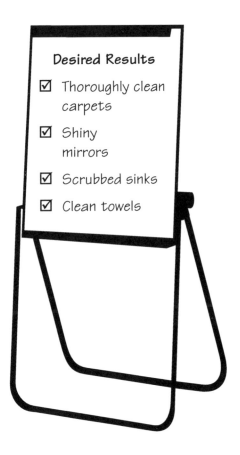

Desired Results

☑ Thoroughly clean carpets

☑ Shiny mirrors

☑ Scrubbed sinks

☑ Clean towels

"In other words let's discuss . . .

our learning objectives." Miriam looked up. *"Please explain that in everyday language."* Rachael smiled. *"No problem."* She flipped over a page on the chart, and wrote *"Thoroughly Clean Carpets"* on the sheet. *"This is one result you and your customers want. Now, what will the employees have to actually do to get this result?"*

"I get it," George said. *"Well, they'll have to vacuum."* Thea jumped in with, *"Not just vacuum, but vacuum everywhere—under the bed and all around the edges of the room."* *"And what about spot cleaning stains?"* Miriam asked.

"Good start," Rachael replied. *"Those are all learning objectives. The housekeeping personnel will need to learn the correct way to vacuum the entire room and effectively spot clean any visible stains. Let's go through the complete list of results this same way."* By the end of the session, the team had identified a number of learning objectives. . . .

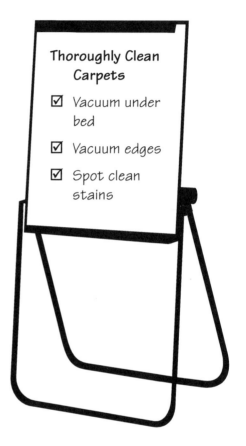

Thoroughly Clean Carpets
- ☑ Vacuum under bed
- ☑ Vacuum edges
- ☑ Spot clean stains

Once you've located where you want training to take you, you have to think about who training will affect.

Considering Your Trainees

Before you choose your training approach, you have to consider your trainees. This step of mapping the training approach involves analyzing those you'll transport in your training vehicle. Elderly passengers might not fare well in a Porsche, and a school bus would be too large for a group of three. Choosing the best mode of transportation requires that you know whom you're hauling.

For example, if your group of trainees consists of fairly young, entry-level employees who need to learn a new software program, you'd try to incorporate a lot of practical, hands-on training that isn't too technical.

Trainee Demographics Matrix

The following Trainee Demographics Matrix is a tool you can use to analyze your trainees. It will help you select the most appropriate training strategies for your participants. Add or delete categories that fit your particular situation. For example, you might not need to know your trainees' math skills. Conversely, you may want to include the male/female ratio, attitudes, biases, physical characteristics, cultural mix, skills your trainees may/may not have mastered, or anything else that may affect your training.

TRAINEE DEMOGRAPHICS MATRIX

Organization/Division: _____

Training Program: _____

Trainee Group	Demographics					
	Education	Math Skills	Language Skills	Age	Motivation	Historical Data

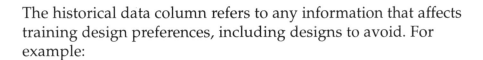
The historical data column refers to any information that affects training design preferences, including designs to avoid. For example:

☑ Will there be many distractions for this group of trainees (e.g., phone calls, interruptions to take care of "business," etc.)? Make sure that expectations are clear up front regarding interruptions.

☑ Employees may feel pressured to get "real" work done as training proceeds and may start showing up late, taking extended breaks, etc. You need to be sensitive to this while reinforcing the need for training.

☑ Do include many extra exercises for fast learners. You don't want them getting bored or "tuning out."

☑ Avoid on-line demonstrations that don't have trainees keying along with the trainer.

☑ Etc.

The Trainee Demographics Matrix will help you get a good grip on your target audience—the employees who will participate in the training. It's essential that you understand them so that the approach you choose for training is best.

Rachael asked for help from the group . . .

in filling out the Trainee Demographics Matrix. *"I don't know the housekeeping personnel,"* she said. *"You do. I need your insight. This tool will help us design a training approach that fits the needs of the employees."* The results proved interesting.

The training team uncovered a mix of personnel. Of the thirty-six individuals in the department, six held supervisory positions. Eight percent *(3 individuals)* were male; 92% *(33 individuals)* were female. Most of the personnel fell into three categories: college students who worked both part and full-time, older women with grammar or high-school education who worked both part- and full-time, and non-English speaking women *(primarily full-time)* with lower educational levels and ages ranging from 17-60 years. Here is part of their Trainee Demographics Matrix. . . .

TRAINEE DEMOGRAPHICS MATRIX

Organization/Division: Smithton Hotel

Training Program: Cleaning Guest Rooms

Trainee Group	Demographics					
	Education	Math Skills	Language Skills	Age	Motivation	Historical Data
College Students	Some College	Good	Good	18-24	Work Experience and Money	Fast Learners
Older Women	Grammar or H.S.	Medium	Good	50-65	Money	Learn By Doing
Non-English Speaking Women	Grammar or H.S.	Medium	Poor	17-60	Money	Need Translator Learn By Doing

The training team felt that the employees . . .

could be motivated by money, especially since most of the positions were entry-level. *"I'm trying to make ends meet at home,"* was a typical attitude.

An incentive program was currently in force, and all agreed to keep it—if it was tied to how well the employees cleaned the rooms. They felt the connection was essential to successful follow-through after training.

"How else can this information help us design our training?" Rachael asked. *"We'll need a translator,"* George concluded. *"And forget any lectures,"* Thea added. *"They'll go over like a lead balloon. We need practical training."*

"And no offense to you, George," Miriam suggested, *"but make sure the trainer is a woman. Most of us on the staff are women."* *"Oh, come on,"* George responded. *"I wanted to demonstrate how to scrub sinks."* The team laughed, then spent the next half hour discussing the trainees and their specific needs in relation to training. . . .

Once you've placed your potential trainees under your training microscope, you can begin designing your work.

Designing Your Approach

Now comes the quest to choose the right type of vehicle to move your trainees toward their destination. You want a smooth journey. Knowing more about your trainees gives you a competitive edge in designing the best approach for your situation. Think about your trainees as you select which learning methods would be most appropriate.

More than likely, you'll be concerned with . . . *"What is the most effective method for getting the content across to participants?"* Ten common learning methods and their descriptions follow.

TEN COMMON LEARNING METHODS	
Lecture	Delivery of content by the trainer.
Structured Discussion	Structured conversations between participants *(in small or large groups)*, aimed toward specific learning objectives.
Panel Discussion	Short lectures or discussion by a variety of trainers *(or guests)*, rather than a single trainer.
Reading	Individual reading of participant materials during a structured time frame.
Case Study	Written description of a situation which contains enough details so participants can discuss specific recommendations.
Role Play	Re-enactment of a specific situation by the participants who are provided with made-up role descriptions.
Skill Application	Re-enactment of a specific situation by participants who create their own on-the-job situations they are currently facing.
Simulation	Elaborate description of a situation which contains carefully programmed decision points and is evaluated *(or experienced)* by *"teams"* of participants.
Games	Challenging activities which engage participants to solve something or *"compete"* with one another.
Personal Action Planning	Identifying specific activities that the participant is committing to carry out back on the job.

The advantages and disadvantages of common learning methods are listed in the Appendix. Because you know your trainees better than any outsider, it's your call as to which methods will work in your situation.

> ## The planning team at Smithton Hotel . . .
> was certain of which methods wouldn't work. Thea had already crossed out lectures, and reading would be cumbersome at best, especially since the educational levels varied greatly. Rachael steered the group toward some of the participative methods, including discussions, role plays, skill applications, and games. All agreed that those methods could work. *"I think the personal action planning is a good idea, too,"* Miriam suggested. *"What if we draw up a checklist of the tasks involved in cleaning a room during the training? Each individual could refer to that list while cleaning."* . . .

After you come to a consensus on which learning methods to use, you have to choose the types of training that will work best. What will work for your trainees in your organization? One-on-one training? Small groups? Classroom training? Or maybe you have the resources to design computer-based training.

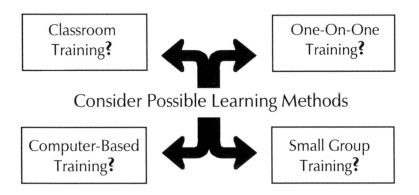

Use the following Learning Methods Checklist. It will help you consider which types of training will work for you. Remember, you're not limited to one method. You might decide, for example, to utilize videotapes in classroom training for one day, then switch to self-instructed training after that.

LEARNING METHODS CHECKLIST

Do I have . . .	1-On-1 Training	Small Group Training	Class-room Training	Self-Instructed Training	Video-tapes	CBT	Job-aids	Etc.
1. Adequate development time?								
2. Adequate program budget?								
3. Adequate resources: equipment and materials for development?								
4. Adequate staff and skills for this type of program?								
5. Appropriate learning environment and equipment?								
6. Appropriate instructional design *(given audience and targeted learning domains)?*								
7. Ease of update with this medium?								
8. Opportunities for repeated use?								
9. Opportunities for integration with other programs?								
10. Will this medium work in our output-driven culture?								
TOTALS								

The training team crossed videotapes . . .

and CBT off their list immediately. *"Developing videotapes in two languages would take too much time, and computers won't help our cause,"* George decided. The others chimed in with their ideas, until finally the group reached a decision—small-group training. This approach will allow them to schedule sessions at different times and to group the non-English speakers together.

LEARNING METHODS CHECKLIST								
Do I have . . .	1-On-1 Training	Small Group Training	Class-room Training	Self-Instructed Training	Video-tapes		Job-aids	Etc.
1. Adequate development time?	✔	✔		✔			✔	
2. Adequate program budget?		✔	✔	✔				
3. Adequate resources: equipment and materials for development?		✔						
4. Adequate staff and skills for this type of program?		✔	✔	✔				
5. Appropriate learning environment and equipment?	✔	✔						
6. Appropriate instructional design *(given audience and targeted learning domains)?*	✔	✔					✔	

Selecting the appropriate learning methods and choosing the types of training are both part of mapping your approach. And they conclude this phase of the High-IMPACT Training Model. The next phase is the last to precede the actual training. Read on to discover how to produce effective learning tools!

CHAPTER FIVE WORKSHEET:
TESTING YOUR TRAINING APPROACH

1. Identify a result you would like your training to achieve.

_____

_____

_____

2. Come up with learning objectives that will help you reach that desired result.

a. _____

b. _____

c. _____

3. In one paragraph, describe your trainees.

_____

_____

_____

_____

_____

_____

4. Look at the following list of ten learning methods. Place a check by each one that could possibly work in your training effort.

☐ Lecture   ☐ Role Play

☐ Structured Discussion   ☐ Skill Application

☐ Panel Discussion   ☐ Simulation

☐ Reading   ☐ Games

☐ Case Study   ☐ Personal Action Planning

5. Refer to the Learning Methods Checklist in this chapter. What types of training would work in your situation? List them.

_____

_____

_____

_____

_____

_____

_____

PRODUCING EFFECTIVE LEARNING TOOLS

Once you've pinpointed the training objectives and approach that will work best for your trainees, you can tackle the development of your learning tools. You've identified your destination and chosen your mode of transportation. Now you have to equip your vehicle with the options that will make your ride easier. Doing so will maximize the learning process.

Linking Learning To The Senses

If your goal is to make learning easier and more effective for your trainees, it's essential to understand the means through which people learn—the senses. A person's senses provide the channels through which information flows. In addition, learning theorists say that people master knowledge, concepts, and skills through *"certain senses"* more than others.

This correlation between learning and the senses can be charted as follows:

THIS PERCENT OF LEARNING . . .		OCCURS THROUGH THIS SENSE . . .
80%		Sight
10%		Hearing
5%		Touch
5%		Smell/Taste

The more that the senses are stimulated, the more people learn. Avoid plain lectures unaccompanied by visual aids. Information presented through program materials that simultaneously use both words and pictures is seven times more likely to be retained than words alone. Similarly, details are much more likely to be remembered if training involves a high degree of structure *(as opposed to a loose, informal learning experience).*

So why is this phase an important one in the creation of high-impact training? Because producing effective learning tools can increase the learning potential of your trainees. The more they learn, the better their chances of improving their job performance. And improved job performance eventually leads to organizational impact. It's the ripple effect in action.

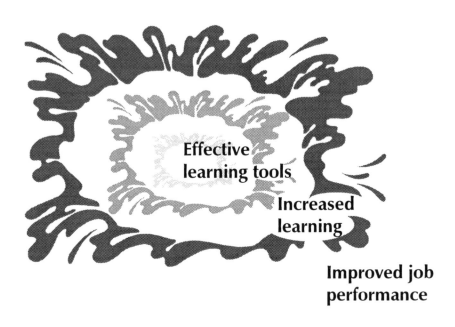

Selecting Program Materials

When you mapped the training approach in the previous chapter, you had to take a good look at your trainees. That analysis enabled

you to choose an approach tailored to them. In this phase, you'll use that analysis again to select your program materials.

Consider your range of program materials, the learning environment available to your trainees, and your trainees' level of expertise. For example, if you have the resources, time, and equipment available to produce comprehensive printed material, but few of your trainees read, it wouldn't be a good choice.

Or suppose you'd like to produce overheads, but the only room available isn't large enough to squeeze in a projector and a screen? Choosing the right learning tools requires a careful evaluation of all your parameters.

Use the following Program Material Checklist to help you decide upon learning tools that fit your trainees and your situation.

PROGRAM MATERIAL CHECKLIST								
Do I have . . .	Flip Charts	Over-heads	Slides	Printed Materials	Video-tapes	Computer Projection	Model	Etc.
1. Adequate development time?								
2. Adequate program budget?								
3. Adequate resources: equipment and materials for development?								
4. Adequate staff and skills for this type of program?								
5. Appropriate learning environment and equipment?								
6. Appropriate instructional design (given audience and targeted learning domains)?								
7. Ease of update with this medium?								
8. Opportunities for repeated use?								
9. Opportunities for integration with other programs?								
10. Will this medium work in our output-driven culture?								
TOTALS								

Check each learning tool to see if it fulfills your expectations. Add up the check marks and look carefully at the tools that received the highest marks. Consider using them.

Rachael led the group . . .

in a discussion of the various learning tools. *"We've already decided against videotapes and computer projection,"* she began, *"but the other tools are up for discussion. Didn't we agree on including a personal action plan?"* Thea asked. *"That would fall under printed material, wouldn't it?"* Rachael nodded.

Since price and time were prime considerations, the training team finally decided upon also using overheads and flip charts. The overheads would have to be simple, but the team felt that the combination of tools would help the trainees learn what they needed to learn. Here is a portion of their Program Material Checklist.

PROGRAM MATERIAL CHECKLIST								
Do I have . . .	Flip Charts	Over-heads	Slides	Printed Materials	Video-tapes	Computer Projection	Model	Etc.
1. Adequate development time?	✔	✔	✔	✔			✔	
2. Adequate program budget?	✔	✔		✔			✔	
3. Adequate resources: equipment and materials for development?	✔	✔		✔				
4. Adequate staff and skills for this type of program?		✔	✔	✔				
5. Appropriate learning environment and equipment?	✔	✔	✔	✔				
6. Appropriate instructional design *(given audience and targeted learning domains)*?	✔	✔		✔			✔	

Characteristics of effective program materials

Your choice of program materials is the first step in creating quality materials. But saying you want to include overheads and actually creating quality overheads are two different things.

How do you create effective program materials? Here are some basic characteristics to bear in mind.

CHARACTERISTICS OF EFFECTIVE PROGRAM MATERIALS	
Visible	◆ Can be easily seen ◆ Can be easily read
Simple	◆ Content is digestible, limited ◆ Key words and concepts are highlighted
Accurate	◆ Information is up-to-date, factual, properly ordered, and complete ◆ If revisions are done, all program materials reflect the changes
Interesting	◆ Colors, overlays, illustrations, and layouts attract attention ◆ Design promotes retention
Practical	◆ Program can be *"easily identified with"* from the trainee's point of view ◆ Tools provided are *"application-oriented"* and easy to understand

Determining The Contents

Program materials that meet quality standards are usually quite visual. Creating visual materials is of value whenever your goal is to communicate to another person—be that one person or one thousand. In other words, you will almost always benefit from highly visual programs!

When you set out to plan the specific content that you'd like to present in a visual format, it's helpful to make a rough sketch of each visual.

That way you can better arrange the text and illustrations, as well as review them all together to decide whether or not they flow appropriately. Whether you use a *"storyboard"* planning guide similar to the one that follows, 3" x 5" cards, or sheets of flipchart paper, focus on the following items:

☑ Title: **Be action-oriented**, and convey the topic.

☑ Key Points: **Highlight critical concepts** or content that trainees need to remember. Limit the amount of content in order to *"keep it simple."*

☑ Layout: **Emphasize main points graphically** with bullets, bold type, colors, etc. Incorporate illustrations, diagrams, cartoons, frames, etc. as needed to add impact.

STORYBOARD PLANNING GUIDE

Program Title: _____   Page _____ of _____

	Key Points	Layout
Title: _____	_____	
_____	_____	
_____	
Type: _____	_____	
_____	

Title: _____	_____	
_____	_____	
_____	
Type: _____	_____	
_____	

Title: _____	_____	
_____	_____	
_____	
Type: _____	_____	
_____	

Title: _____	_____	
_____	_____	
_____	
Type: _____	_____	
_____	

Title: _____	_____	
_____	_____	
_____	
Type: _____	_____	
_____	

Rachael handed each team member . . .

a Storyboard Planning Guide. *"This will work quite well for our situation,"* she said. *"Each visual can cover a different area of cleaning that the guests expect."* Miriam looked up. *"Do you mean that we'll have separate pictures for the sinks and mirrors?"* The team members laughed. *"You've got the right idea,"* Rachael said. *"Let's begin with the carpets."*

"What about 'Thoroughly Vacuum Carpets' for our title?" George suggested. *"Okay,"* Rachael said. *"Anyone have any ideas for the key points?" "Sure,"* Thea answered. *"We discussed those at the first meeting. We have to vacuum every speck, even under the beds. We need to use the edge nozzle around the edges of the room. And then we have to spot clean the stains."*

"Good start," Rachael replied. *"We can include those ideas on the layout, too. Is anyone up to drawing some pictures?"* George tried his hand at it, then decided to give Miriam a turn. *"Why don't we each fill out the guide for a separate cleaning segment,"* Rachael suggested. *"After we're done, we can look at the different ideas."* The group went to work. . . .

STORYBOARD PLANNING GUIDE

Program Title: __Cleaning Guest Rooms__   Page __1__ of __6__

	Key Points	Layout
Title: __Thoroughly__ __Vacuum Carpets__ Type: __Overhead__	Middle room Edges room Under beds Heavy traffic areas 3 times	 Thoroughly Vacuum Carpets
Title: __Hang Fresh__ __Towels Neatly__ Type: __Overhead__	Two per person Square edges Matching colors Centered Bath mat	 Hang Fresh Towels Neatly

Focusing On The Development Process

Once you've determined the content of your program materials, you can begin the actual creation process. Remember that the goal of this development process is to create materials that are visible, simple, accurate, interesting, and practical.

Guidelines for the most common program materials are given on the pages that follow. You may have heard some of these tips before; others will be new to you. They all will help you in your quest to produce effective learning tools.

FLIP CHARTS PROCESS GUIDELINES

→ Consider using two flip charts so you can develop ideas in tandem *(one chart, pre-prepared, and the second one, blank, for spontaneous notes).*

→ Write LARGE *(2 to 3 inch lettering)* with a broadtipped felt pen. Water-based pens *"bleed through"* less than permanent ink types, and save paper!

→ Write on every other page, especially when pre-preparing a flip chart. This will not only reduce *"bleed through,"* but will also keep topics *"unseen"* until you are ready to present them to participants.

→ Use several colors of pens for variety and to highlight specific points *(red with blue, green with black, blue or red with black, etc.).*

→ Try writing notes lightly in hard pencil on the flip chart to assist you in your presentation. *(They generally cannot be seen, even from the front row.)*

→ Make tabs out of masking tape or small "Post-It®" type notes. Adhere to the edges of the chart paper so that you can easily turn to a prepared page.

→ Prepare for *"revealing points one at a time"* by taping pieces of paper or cardboard over words to *"reveal."*

OVERHEADS PROCESS GUIDELINES

→ Paraphrase carefully; keep it simple by limiting key points and bullets.

→ Use a clean character font in 18 points or larger, and in upper/lower case.

→ Check the legibility from a distance.

→ A rule of thumb: One-inch lettering is typically visible at 30 feet, two-inch at 60 feet, etc.

→ A suggestion: Make the blank space between lines 1½ times the letter height.

→ Don't make the overhead too busy with too many colors.

→ Try mounting the overheads in cardboard frames *(notes can be written on the frames)* or use clear top-loading plastic sheet protectors not only to protect, but also to make handling easier.

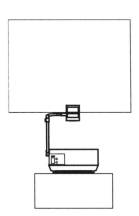

→ Keep your *"style"* consistent throughout the program.

→ Consider making handouts of your overheads to reduce note-taking during the presentation.

SLIDES PROCESS GUIDELINES

→ Use only one main idea per slide with a maximum of 15 or 16 words per slide.

→ Utilize simple charts/graphs *(tables are confusing)*, and format with upper/lower case letters.

→ Combine graphics with words for maximum impact, effectiveness.

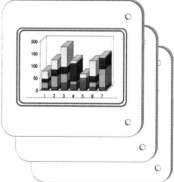

→ Design for a dark background *(the effect will look stronger, cleaner)*, and don't use too many colors.

→ Don't mix vertical and horizontal slides *(if possible)*.

→ Edit the slide presentation to ensure correct ordering, positioning, and presentation pace.

→ Keep your *"style"* consistent throughout the slide show.

PRINTED MATERIALS PROCESS GUIDELINES

→ Make sure that all content is complete, accurate, and in the correct order. *(Tabs and page numbering make information more accessible.)*

→ De-emphasize the use of *"to be;"* instead use active verbs.

→ Create parallel structures, yet vary sentence structures to capture and retain attention.

→ Use graphics, diagrams, and guided notes to highlight key concepts and content. *(Also, consider using color when feasible.)*

→ Leave plenty of white space; this makes the print materials more inviting and easier to read. *(Clean, clear fonts also help readability.)*

→ Allow plenty of room *(structure or unstructured)* for note-taking.

→ Customize the language, title, and content to the audience *(whether individuals or groups)*, and produce materials cleanly *(dark even ink, printed straight not skewed)* on quality paper.

VIDEOTAPE DEVELOPMENT GUIDELINES

→ Include nine key development steps in the pre-production phase:

❶ Problem or need identification

❷ Objectives

❸ Audience analysis

❹ Budgeting/scheduling

❺ Research

❻ Scripting

❼ Resources/props

❽ Talent

❾ Rehearsal

→ Include three key developmental steps in the production phase:

❶ Graphics

❷ Narration/soundtrack

❸ Shooting

→ Include four key developmental steps in the post-production phase:

❶ Editing

❷ Duplication

❸ Distribution

❹ Evaluation

→ Attract the ear:

◆ Loud sounds more than soft

◆ Musical sounds more than noise

◆ Sounds that match picture

VIDEOTAPE DEVELOPMENT GUIDELINES *(continued)*

→ Attract the eye:

◆ Moving images more than stationary images

◆ Bright images more than dark

◆ Colored images more than pastel or gray

◆ Dynamic balance more than formal balance

◆ Human faces more than patterns

◆ Patterns more than random noise

◆ Smooth shot continuity more than disjointed arrangements

→ Capture the viewer and deliver the message:

◆ Talent becomes the message, must be credible with viewers

◆ Light creates dimension *(always control)*; provides information, shape, texture, spatial orientation, level of importance, time, mood, etc.

◆ Sound/music creates mood, ambiance, realism to scene; adds to message, highlights and strengthens scene, helps with transitions, helps provide a space, time, and situation

◆ Screen position should always emphasize subject, control content and flow, control movement, strengthen message composition . . . formal and balanced, or dynamic and unbalanced

After you've chosen and created effective learning tools, you're ready to embark on the actual training itself. The next chapter provides techniques that help trainers achieve success.

CHAPTER SIX WORKSHEET: CHOOSING EFFECTIVE LEARNING TOOLS

Using the Program Material Checklist on the next page, begin selecting media materials for a program you're currently planning.

1. List your top choices. Why did you choose these materials?

_____

_____

_____

_____

_____

_____

_____

_____

_____

_____

_____

_____

_____

PROGRAM MATERIAL CHECKLIST

Do I have . . .	Flip Charts	Over-heads	Slides	Printed Materials	Video-tapes	Computer Projection	Model	Etc.
1. Adequate development time?								
2. Adequate program budget?								
3. Adequate resources: equipment and materials for development?								
4. Adequate staff and skills for this type of program?								
5. Appropriate learning environment and equipment?								
6. Appropriate instructional design (given audience and targeted learning domains)?								
7. Ease of update with this medium?								
8. Opportunities for repeated use?								
9. Opportunities for integration with other programs?								
10. Will this medium work in our output-driven culture?								
TOTALS								

APPLYING SUCCESSFUL TRAINING TECHNIQUES

Training looms ahead. You've identified the need for your trip, decided upon your destination, chosen your vehicle, and equipped it with all the essentials for an easy ride. You're ready to load up your passengers and begin training. But wait. The success of your journey also hinges upon the person you've hired to drive.

Does he know how to shift? Can she maneuver around debris on the road? Does he know how to use his rearview mirror? In other words, is your trainer *(whether that's you or someone else)* successful at training? You wouldn't want to place an expensive car in the hands of an inexperienced driver.

This analogy may seem a bit farfetched—but think about it. You've spent a good many hours or days *(or even months in some cases)* preparing and planning for your training effort. An effective trainer will put that time to good use. An ineffective trainer may dump it down the drain.

If you're concerned about how well you'll be able to steer your training sessions, read through the tips and techniques that follow. They may provide you with some new ideas that you can put to use in the midst of either coaching individuals or facilitating groups.

Employing Successful Delivery Skills

No one is exempt from improving their delivery skills. Even the greatest speakers continually strive to increase their effectiveness.

And for good reason. Learning can only occur if your audience hears and understands what you are trying to get across.

In order to really communicate with your trainees, you must skillfully incorporate a variety of delivery skills *(both verbal and nonverbal)*. Your goal is to facilitate learning—to interest, unite, maybe even excite the individuals you're coaching. To that end, you must learn to be aware of not only *what* content you are delivering, but also *how* you are delivering it.

Verbal delivery skills

As a trainer *(or coach/facilitator)*, you have a great tool at your disposal—your voice! If you desire to use your voice to its best advantage, you should attempt to develop a voice that can be described as follows:

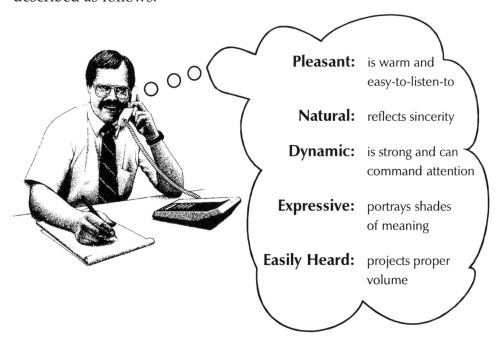

Pleasant: is warm and easy-to-listen-to

Natural: reflects sincerity

Dynamic: is strong and can command attention

Expressive: portrays shades of meaning

Easily Heard: projects proper volume

If you're unsure of how your voice sounds in a training situation, tape record or videotape yourself. You can also ask for feedback from an objective source. Ask that person to comment on your voice in light of the five key characteristics of an effective speaking voice. Then, practice. Practice is instrumental in improving your speaking voice.

Nonverbal delivery skills

Your voice isn't the only tool you can use to your advantage. Using your body can also add emphasis and clarity to your words. If you want to convince your trainees of your sincerity, depth of

knowledge, confidence, and enthusiasm—learn to utilize nonverbal delivery skills.

Individuals pick up visual messages in your posture, hand gestures, body movements, facial expressions, and eye contact. You can't prevent sending nonverbal messages, but you certainly can learn to manage and control them.

How? Let's look at the different nonverbal cues you can send.

Posture

Posture reflects your attitude. If you're speaking to a large group, stand tall and confidently. If you are seated while coaching an individual or small group, sit up straight.

Hand gestures

Hand gestures reinforce a verbal message or convey a particular thought or emotion. To use gestures effectively:

➜ Respond naturally to what you think, feel, and say

➜ Match the action to the words and the situation

➜ Use gestures that are pleasing and convincing

➜ Ensure that your gestures are smooth and well-timed

Body movements

The key point to remember about body movement is to *"never move without a reason."* The eye is attracted to a moving object, so any full-body movements you make during a training session invite attention.

Facial expressions

Participants typically watch a trainer's face during a session. They will usually look to your face for evidence of confidence, friendliness, and sincerity.

Strange as it sounds, the first step toward projecting these qualities is to recognize expressions that don't belong on your face. If you discover, for example, that you tend to frown, you can then work toward controlling that expression through disciplined practice.

Eye contact

Eye contact is the cohesive element that bonds trainers with the individuals they are training. You can use your eyes to interest and involve participants. Some strategies for establishing effective eye contact include:

→ Know your material so you don't have to rely on notes.

→ Focus your eyes for a few seconds on individual participants throughout the session.

→ Use your eyes to actively seek out nonverbal feedback from the trainees.

Nonverbal delivery skills can also improve with practice. A videotape of your practice or of your performance in an actual training situation will provide you with invaluable information. Use it to assess your skills and to determine where you need to improve.

The training team decided . . .

that Rachael, as the corporate trainer, would lead the small-group training sessions. However, Rachael thought it would be advantageous if both Miriam and Thea helped demonstrate the skills. George also asked Rosa, a bilingual employee in the department, to join the team so she could help train the Spanish-speaking employees.

Miriam was especially nervous. *"I'll work with you,"* Rachael offered. So she had George videotape the two of them while they practiced a session. Together, Rachael and Miriam identified a couple of areas Miriam could practice—the projection of her voice and her hand gestures. *"It's normal to speak softly when you're nervous,"* Rachael said. *"And we can work together so that your hand gestures aren't too jittery."*

During the first session, Miriam still spoke too softly. But she showed improvement during the second; and, after the third, both she and Rachael were pleased with her performance. . . .

Using Support Materials Effectively

Producing effective learning tools, as you did in the previous chapter, is only half the battle. You also have to use them effectively.

What if you can't show your terrific overheads because the bulb is burned out in the overhead projector and you don't have a spare? What if your trainees can't see the flipchart because you're blocking their view?

The following guidelines will help you use your learning tools effectively, which will expand your effectiveness as a trainer.

Flipcharts

◆ Write rapidly and legibly; don't be afraid to misspell or abbreviate words.

◆ Talk as you write and face the audience when possible. *(Don't hesitate to ask for assistance in turning pages or writing.)*

◆ Use color *(and/or a pencil or pen as a pointer)* to retain attention.

◆ Tear off sheets and post them around the room when appropriate, using masking tape only *(other tape can damage walls)*.

◆ Use symbols, circles, and underlines to help separate ideas and highlight key concepts.

Overheads

◆ Demonstrate how to complete an actual sample form with the group using overhead pens. Overlay one on another to show a diagram developed in sequence, a completed worksheet, or an evolving flow chart.

◆ Use a sheet of paper to allow you to reveal a portion of the transparency while temporarily blocking out the rest.

◆ Use your pencil as a pointer to emphasize detail.

◆ Check that the overhead projector has an extra bulb and that you know how to replace it.

◆ Avoid becoming a part of the transparency *(e.g., having a portion of the overhead projection appear on you, etc.).*

Slides

◆ Preview the slides shortly before the session to ensure they are ready to use *(none upside down or backward)* when you need them.

◆ Follow your presentation plan, sharing pre-rehearsed key points for each slide.

◆ Speak with more volume than you normally use. *(As with other media, the listener's attention is divided, and in a darkened room, more volume will help hold attention.)*

◆ Use a remote control to allow you to move during the training.

◆ Vary the pace of slides being presented, making sure not to *"flash"* too quickly and not to *"hold"* for too long. *(An average = 15 to 20 seconds per slide.)* Also, break the presentation into shorter segments of 5 or 6 slides.

Print material

◆ Familiarize yourself with the print materials before distributing them to the learners.

◆ Use a highlighter to mark key points you will want to share with the participants.

◆ Point out structural information that will make the program more accessible.

◆ Provide reproducibles for on-the-job use.

◆ Distribute print materials at appropriate times.

Videotapes

◆ Preview the videotape again just prior to using it in a training session.

◆ *"Cue"* videotapes so they are *"ready to roll"* when used, rather than causing the participants to view several minutes of blank screen.

◆ Provide an appropriate level of lighting which allows participants to take notes if they wish.

◆ Play the video at the appropriate volume.

◆ Pause the videotape during appropriate points to encourage discussion; it's an excellent way to actively involve participants.

Thea thought the tips . . .

on using the overhead projector were great. *"I would have become part of the material if you hadn't reminded me to stay away from the projection,"* she told Rachael after her first session. And since Rachael had Rosa double-check the personal action plans written in Spanish, they were able to identify errors that they could correct before the sessions began. . . .

Fielding Questions

Your ability to field questions effectively can make or break your training session. What if you don't know how to answer a technical question that comes up? What if someone asks an important question, but you don't think it should be addressed until later? The following suggestions should prove helpful in fielding such questions.

☞ **Repeat or rephrase the question**

This ensures that all participants hear it, it gives you additional time to think about your response, and it allows you an opportunity to restate the question in more favorable terms.

☞ **Receive all questions cordially**

Remain courteous and agreeable. Maintaining your composure is crucial to effectively fielding questions.

☞ **Evaluate the relevance of the question**

If it's relevant, respond accordingly. If not, consider giving a brief explanation, then inviting the trainee to speak with you privately after the session.

☞ **Always address a question**

Do respond to every question. If you don't know the answer, say, *"I don't know, but I'll find out for you."*

☞ **Be brief**

It's not good practice to break the continuity of a presentation with lengthy answers. Be as brief as you can while still providing a complete answer that is acceptable to the questioner.

At the beginning . . .

of one of the small-group sessions, Cory, a college student who worked part-time, interrupted Rachael with, *"Why do we even need this training? We were trained when we were hired."* Rachael stopped to respond. *"I can see that you're interested in discovering why we're conducting these sessions. That's a good question."* She paused, then continued by explaining the need for training. Her response defused Cory's attack.

Each training situation is different. However, if you learn to employ successful verbal and nonverbal delivery skills, utilize program materials effectively, and competently field questions, you'll earn your right to be in the training driver's seat.

CHAPTER SEVEN WORKSHEET:
EXAMINING TRAINING TECHNIQUES

1. Consider your most recent training experience.

    a. Describe the trainer's verbal skills.

    _____

    _____

    b. Describe the trainer's nonverbal skills.

    _____

    _____

    c. Could the trainer have improved either of these skills? If yes, explain.

    _____

    _____

2. Choose one learning tool that you use frequently (*e.g., overheads, slides, flipcharts, videotapes, etc.*). Having read the guidelines for use, have you learned to do anything differently? If so, what?

    _____

    _____

CALCULATING MEASURABLE TRAINING RESULTS

The training sessions are over. Your vehicle has come to a halt. You open the door, let your passengers out, and thank them for coming along. But while the ride is over, your journey isn't complete. You have to determine the success of your training effort. Did your passengers enjoy the ride? Did you take them the entire way to the correct destination?

You'll be put to the test when it comes to proving the value of your training effort. While you need to look at each training effort on a case-by-case basis, complete measurement involves calculating the following:

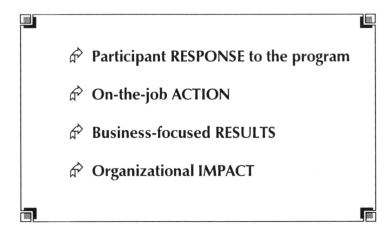

🖋 **Participant RESPONSE to the program**

🖋 **On-the-job ACTION**

🖋 **Business-focused RESULTS**

🖋 **Organizational IMPACT**

These measures ensure that training is value-added and aligned with your organization's goals.

Evaluating Program RESPONSE

To successfully evaluate program RESPONSE, you need to figure in two kinds of training responses: *"Response to"* + *"Response from."*

"Response to" refers to the participants' reactions to the program. For example:

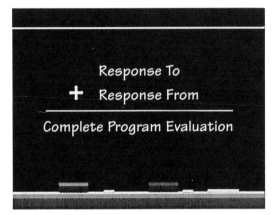

- **9** Did the trainees find the program design and learning materials appropriate, interesting, and usable?

- **9** Did they find the facilitator knowledgeable, helpful, motivating, etc.?

"Response from" the training is defined through participants' learning. Did the training actually result in learning? Quantitative *"response from"* measurements include evaluation tools like:

→ Pre-Tests/Post-Tests

→ Skill Demonstrations

→ Simulation Certification

Qualitative *"response from"* measures tell how participants view their own learning. Use *questionnaires* and *interview guides* for qualitative responses. They're good tools in evaluating whether or not participants feel they have learned the new skills that they were supposed to learn.

It is important to plan for and evaluate both kinds of RESPONSE. Think of it in this way: participants may have enjoyed the program, ranking their *"response to"* the program with high marks, yet if they didn't learn the skills you wanted them to learn, what's the point?

On the other hand, suppose the participants gained new skills as indicated in *"response from"* measurements, but they did not find the instructor or program materials very helpful. Shouldn't you— one of the people responsible for the training—be made aware of this so you can make adjustments? Absolutely. Complete program evaluation is a sum of both RESPONSE measures.

Devise a questionnaire that is tailored to your specific program design and content. An example of a questionnaire that evaluates a trainer is provided in the Appendix. If you wish, use those questions in your questionnaire, adding or deleting items as you see fit.

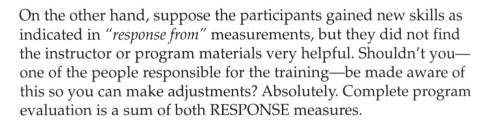

To help you evaluate program RESPONSE, consider the following tips.

☑ TIP 1   **Allow time for evaluation.**

☑ TIP 2   **Create a simple, short evaluation.**

☑ TIP 3   **Don't skew results.**

☑ TIP 4   **Include an evaluation form for the trainer.**

Do communicate the results of your RESPONSE measurements. The participants have a stake in the process. Management is also interested in these initial measurements, so keep them informed.

The initial results of the training sessions . . .

for the housekeeping personnel at Smithton Hotel were quite positive. Questionnaires were handed out at the close of each session, allowing for immediate feedback. The overall rating of the program was *"3.2" (on a scale of 1 to 4).*

Each employee was also asked to demonstrate the various skills taught during the sessions, and was given help if any skill wasn't up to par. For example, if an employee had trouble making the beds correctly, she'd be assigned to one-on-one training with her supervisor. The training team was pleased with the initial results of their training program. . . .

Assessing On-The-Job ACTION

The next step involves finding out what ACTION is taking place back on the job. Will those who participated in your training really apply what they've learned?

If training is to be successful, it must have practical application. Learning new skills or techniques is great, but unless you see that learning put into action, it has no value. Assessing on-the-job ACTION gives evidence that your training is worthwhile.

Subordinates   **Supervisors**

Trainees   **Peers**

Multi-source input

In assessing what ACTION is being taken back on the job, you should survey those who are directly involved with the ACTION. This means you'll be securing input from multiple sources, which often involves surveying those who completed the training and their supervisors.

But what if the training you are addressing involves a skill such as change management, effective leadership, or team-building? Then, you'll probably want to survey the training participants and their supervisors, plus the training participants' subordinates and peers.

Each training effort will be different, so you need to decide who should provide input into the ACTION assessment. Surveying all parties involved with or affected by the ACTION creates multi-source input. Multi-source input creates better, balanced evaluations.

ACTION assessment

Once you know who you want to survey, you need to decide <u>how</u> you will survey them. Among your choices are:

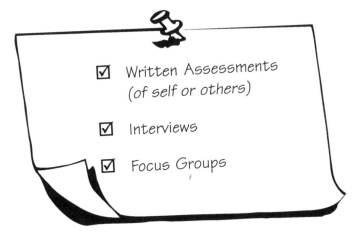

☑ Written Assessments
(of self or others)

☑ Interviews

☑ Focus Groups

Decide which kind of survey form will work best for your organization. Then, implement it.

> ### One month after the housekeeping personnel . . .
> had completed their training sessions, Rachael and George distributed survey forms to each participant and to all the supervisors. Supervisors were told to evaluate their employees as a group. All answers would be kept strictly confidential. The surveys revealed that the employees were using their new skills, although full-time employees were doing better than the part-timers. . . .

You can effectively use these kinds of surveys in three ways.

❶ First, you can compare this ACTION assessment to the previous RESPONSE evaluation to see if there is a link between the participants' responses and their actions.

❷ Second, you can find out if the trainees are applying newly learned skills in areas that have been targeted for performance improvement. By doing this second comparison, you can help trainees take ACTION in the areas that count.

❸ Finally, you can continue to use these surveys over an extended period of time to help promote lasting ACTION.

Let the participants know your findings. The value of open communication can't be stressed enough. At this stage in the process, you want the participants to visualize how the training has actually helped them. You also want upper management to realize how the training is improving the organization by affecting on-the-job ACTION.

Analyzing Business-Focused RESULTS

Now it's time to begin analyzing business-focused RESULTS. In general, business-focused RESULTS can be divided into two categories: hard or soft.

"Hard results" are easier to analyze. They are more concrete, objectively observable, and you can usually assign numbers to them easily. The four kinds of measures typically used in analyzing hard results include:

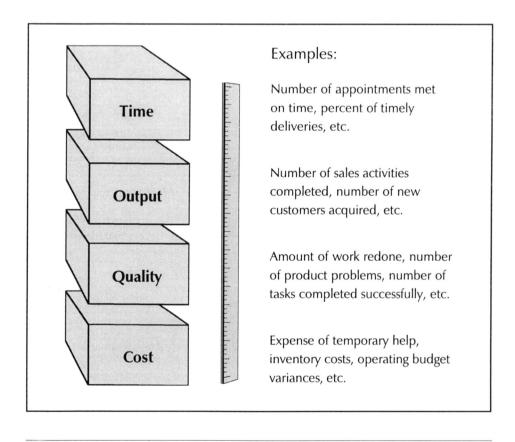

Examples:

Number of appointments met on time, percent of timely deliveries, etc.

Number of sales activities completed, number of new customers acquired, etc.

Amount of work redone, number of product problems, number of tasks completed successfully, etc.

Expense of temporary help, inventory costs, operating budget variances, etc.

"Soft results" can be much more complicated to analyze, because these outcomes are often based on people's behavior and attitudes. However, they *can* be measured, and will lend more credence to the success of your training. Four categories that soft results can be divided into include:

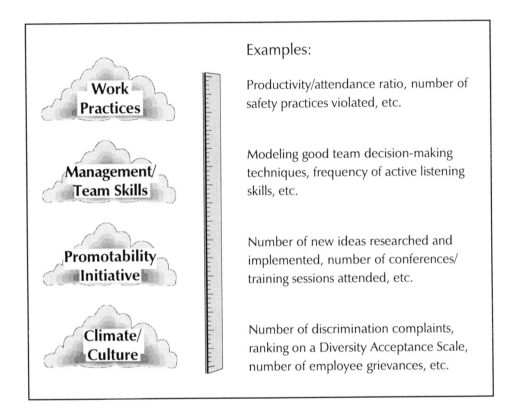

Examples:

Productivity/attendance ratio, number of safety practices violated, etc.

Modeling good team decision-making techniques, frequency of active listening skills, etc.

Number of new ideas researched and implemented, number of conferences/ training sessions attended, etc.

Number of discrimination complaints, ranking on a Diversity Acceptance Scale, number of employee grievances, etc.

To best plan for RESULTS, check that you have identified as many objective measurements as possible. When this is not possible, be aware that your analysis must be qualified.

Careful considerations

As you plan to analyze your RESULTS, take the following tips into consideration.

1. **Use multi-source input**

   To successfully project your business-focused RESULTS, you must obtain input from all the sources that count. It's these multiple sources that can provide input as to which measures are important and how they should be measured.

2. **Measure what counts**

   Whether you're measuring hard or soft skills, the key is to only gather data that you will truly use. In addition, you should measure only when the targeted measurement is really value-added.

3. **Link training to results**

   Can you attribute a high level of business-focused RESULTS to training? Or is that being presumptuous? Don't other factors influence the results?

   Absolutely. But you *can* make an educated estimate of the role training plays in the process.

   Observe what's happening in your organization. If the organization is the same as when your baseline measurements were being tabulated, the connection between RESULTS and training will be strong. Conversely, if your organization has not remained constant, the link will be much weaker and, consequently, harder to prove.

   Clarify the link between your training effort and the resulting outcomes. Use multi-source input, measure what counts, and link training to results. With these three considerations behind you, you're ready to look at the actual RESULTS.

The training team at Smithton Hotel . . .

had identified targeted business results for each of the four *"hard"* measurement categories. These targets represented the major performance areas that needed significant improvement. They listed their targeted outcomes and added a column to include current measurements. Here's a sample of what they discovered. . . .

MEASUREMENT CATEGORY: Quality	PRE-TRAINING BASELINE MEASURE	POST-TRAINING TARGET	POST-TRAINING ACTUAL MEASURE
Housekeeping personnel's adherence to cleanliness standards for rooms as validated by supervisors	6 out of 10 rooms pass inspection as validated by supervisors	9 out of 10	8 out of 10
Customer satisfaction of room cleanliness as reported in comment cards	7.2 on a scale of 1 to 10	9 out of 10	8 out of 10

The Housekeeping Department at Smithton Hotel experienced sizeable gains. Your organization can do the same. **Significant** business-focused RESULTS can be achieved and analyzed. The cumulative sum of these RESULTS will translate into desired IMPACT.

While it's easier to do hard skill analysis, you also can analyze soft-skill RESULTS if you establish appropriate measurements and gather baseline data.

Simply, plug these kinds of measurements into a table like the one the training team at Smithton Hotel used:

MEASUREMENT CATEGORY: Climate Culture	PRE-TRAINING BASELINE MEASURE	POST-TRAINING TARGET	POST-TRAINING ACTUAL MEASURE (9 mos. Post-Training)
Employee ranking of organization on a Diversity Acceptance Scale	4 out of 10 on the Scale	8 out of 10 on the Scale	6 out of 10 on the Scale

RESULT analysis **can be done.** The key? Work toward establishing an objective measurement for each RESULT outcome. With soft skills, that requires some thinking—but you can do it. Plus, remember you're not alone; work in a team, and access multi-source input.

Once again, remember to communicate with the stakeholders of your training effort. Make sure your business-focused RESULT categories and projections reflect departmental input and goals. Then, share your results.

Tracking Organizational IMPACT

You want to demonstrate that your training has IMPACT that will help push your organization ahead in the right direction. While the scope of your training effort may not require—or even justify—a full, *"bottom line"* evaluation, you still can explain how your training contributes to the *"big picture."*

In other words, you may have seen an increase in business-focused RESULTS, but does or will that increase affect your organization positively? If it does, you're right in the ballgame. If it doesn't, your training should never have been scheduled in the first place.

While IMPACT planning is best done before beginning a training effort, it can be carried out later as well. What's important to know is that sometime before or during the tracking of your training's IMPACT, you need to clarify the value of the training effort and project its IMPACT.

Ask the following questions:

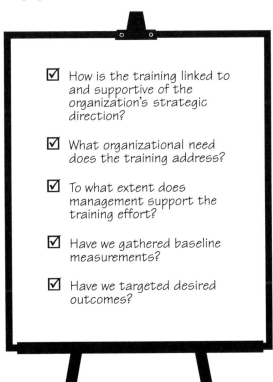

☑ How is the training linked to and supportive of the organization's strategic direction?

☑ What organizational need does the training address?

☑ To what extent does management support the training effort?

☑ Have we gathered baseline measurements?

☑ Have we targeted desired outcomes?

At Smithton Hotel, George, Rachael, and the rest . . .
of the training team had addressed these issues in the beginning. Upper
management saw the need for training and initiated the process. So
management support was present from the start.

The training was implemented to address the problem that customers
had with the cleanliness of the rooms. It was noticeable on the customer
comment cards and was affecting the Customer Satisfaction Index *(CSI)*.
Management felt an improvement had to be made before they lost too
much business. Baseline measurements on the CSI had been gathered and
desired outcomes were targeted.

Tracking guidelines

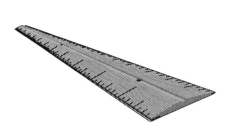

Once you've clarified the value of
your training and projected
IMPACT, follow these guidelines
to help you through this stage of
the measuring process.

❶ Do not promise or claim more of an IMPACT than
the training can actually deliver.

❷ Do have the support of those most directly
affected by the IMPACT outcomes.

❸ Do make clear your IMPACT measuring process.

From the start, be sure to establish:

❓ What is to be measured?

❓ When and for how long you will measure it?

❓ Who does what in the measuring process?

❓ What kinds of calculations will be used to measure it?

Bring in Finance, Accounting, MIS, etc. to help gather baseline data. In addition, measure consistently and for an appropriate length of time. In general, it's best to begin measuring on a monthly basis and chart progress from there. Although you may not see bottom-line IMPACT for quite some time—even a year or more—monthly checking of progress will give you a glimpse of trends and improvements. Finally, when possible, make sure that your IMPACT assessment includes both a Cost/Benefit Analysis and an ROI *(return-on-investment)* calculation.

Evaluating IMPACT may, at times, be quite complex, time-consuming, and even costly, yet it can also be highly informative, rewarding, and value-added. It all depends on your training effort's scope and size.

◆ **Do you need a detailed financial analysis?** *(If so, budgets, variance reports, and a look at various other financial data are in order.)*

—or—

◆ **Do you need to simply provide *"good evidence"* that your training does have IMPACT?**

In either case, report your findings to wrap up the measuring process. Assess what didn't work, what did, and why. Celebrate your success! Also, acknowledge which areas in your training process need improvement. Sharing your IMPACT findings gives your training effort credibility.

If you want your training to be of lasting success, see the next chapter.

CHAPTER EIGHT WORKSHEET: MEASURING YOUR TRAINING RESULTS

1. Based on your RESPONSE evaluation process:

   a. What are some questions you can use to evaluate participant *"response to"* your training?

   _____

   _____

   _____

   b. What tools will you use to evaluate participant learning or *"response from"*?

   ❏ pre-tests/post-tests?   ❏ questionnaires?

   ❏ skill demonstrations?   ❏ interview guides?

   ❏ simulation certification?   ❏ other?

2. What are the top two ACTION objectives for your training effort? List them.

   _____

   _____

   _____

   _____

3. As your training progresses, complete a RESULTS table for your training effort.

MEASUREMENT CATEGORY: _____	PRE-TRAINING BASELINE MEASURE	POST-TRAINING TARGET	POST-TRAINING ACTUAL MEASURE _____

4. Has the value of your training been clearly communicated? If not, what needs to be done to clarify the training effort's value?

_____

_____

_____

TRACKING ONGOING FOLLOW-THROUGH

How can you make sure that training lasts long after the sessions are over? You want your journey to be memorable, to have an impact on those who signed up for the ride. The natural inclination is to let the effects of training slide until you're back to the starting point. But it doesn't have to be that way.

In most training models, there usually is no sixth phase, no concession made for ensuring that the results of training last. Yet this *"follow-through"* phase is critically important in the learning process, just as it is in tennis, golf, and many other areas.

Follow-Through For Success!

And, although it is positioned at the end of the model, it can be factored in much sooner.

You're interested in follow-through if you're committed to training and its potential results. This commitment starts with the basic values and culture of your organization. The following four questions will help you determine the readiness of your organization to make training benefits last.

AM I READY TO MAKE TRAINING BENEFITS LAST?

Are the goals of my organization clear?

Training results have a better chance of lasting if the training objectives are linked to the organization's objectives and become part of the trainees' performance measurements.

Does my organization value improvement?

Training is implemented to bring about improvement in job performance. An organization that values improvement will be interested in lasting training results. Look for signs—Do employees feel encouraged to try new things and to learn?

Does the training budget survive even tough times?

Increasing the impact of a training program requires time and dollars beyond the cost of purchasing or designing a program. The actual follow-through work often takes longer than the training program itself. However, demonstrating impact may help to protect the training budget.

Who is accountable for training results?

You will want to consult with this person about his or her goals and commitment to follow-through. You might need to accept this responsibility yourself.

Preparing For Follow-Through

A few simple preparations on the part of you and the training staff and then the trainees will produce the lasting results that follow-through achieves.

The manager's role in preparation

If you are a manager whose employees will be participating in training . . .

☑ **Decide or clarify how the training will benefit your people, improve their performance, and support your department's objectives.**

Review the training objectives, and visualize in detail how to apply the new skills and ideas.

☑ **Communicate expectations and goals for the training as they relate to follow-through.**

Compare the course objectives with your goals for follow-through and your employees' needs, interests, and expectations. A good match between planned topics, your objectives, and your employees' needs and interests ensures motivation.

☑ **Plan for follow-through practice and feedback activities to reinforce new or changed behaviors.**

One of the best ways to reinforce the application of new skills or procedures is to consider them in goal setting and performance reviews that follow the training.

☑ **Provide input to the training design, as requested. Offer ideas for follow-through.**

You are responsible for finding out about the content of training programs that your employees attend. Sometimes there are opportunities for you to participate in the program design or to review the course in detail prior to its delivery. Take advantage of these opportunities.

The training staff's role in preparation

If you are part of the training staff . . .

☑ **Follow good training program development practices.**

As you develop and review materials, activities, and exercises, consider the desired outcomes of each activity. How will trainees follow-through on them? Does each activity apply to something the trainees need to do, say, or feel back on the job?

☑ **View the trainees' manager as an important internal customer who is crucial to the success of follow-through.**

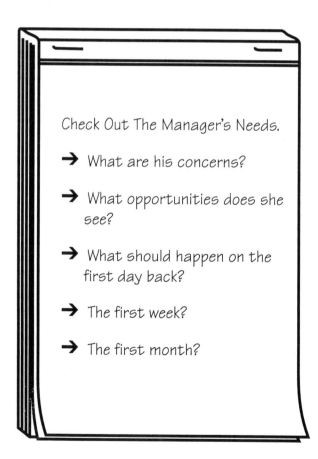

Check Out The Manager's Needs.

→ What are his concerns?

→ What opportunities does she see?

→ What should happen on the first day back?

→ The first week?

→ The first month?

The trainee's role in preparation

If you are a trainee . . .

☑ **Know the purpose for the training and identify several personal benefits.**

If management is not forthcoming with details, ask for them. If training is to help *(and all training is meant to)*, you should have access to the information about how it will actually benefit you.

☑ **Request and review the training agenda. Complete the requested prework.**

The agenda should not be top-secret material. Find out what you'll be learning, and take part in any requests for information, skill tests, etc.

Rachael, an experienced trainer, . . .

knew that forming a training team of people who would be directly involved in and with the training, was essential to the success of the effort. The fact that George, Thea, and Miriam were involved from the beginning helped immensely. And the addition of Rosa in the middle of the training process provided more necessary input. The combined ideas and talents of the various team members upped the program's success rate. . . .

Effective training and successful follow-through require creative thinking and planning on the part of the manager, the training staff, and the trainees. The earlier you address needs for follow-through, the better your chance for success.

Adding Follow-Through To Training

Use the following worksheet as you design or review a proposed training program to ensure that needs for training follow-through have been taken into account.

TYPE OF TRAINING ACTIVITY CHECKLIST

Is this type of activity found in your planned program? If not, could it be added or could a planned activity be modified?

☐ Videos that present situations and styles the participants relate to and are able to recall and visualize later.

☐ Activity debriefs *(reviews)* and discussions that help the trainees pull new ideas together, summarize what they have learned, and help them take the ideas away from the session.

☐ Small-group activities that allow trainees from the same work unit to build a basis for strong follow-through tasks.

☐ Training materials that summarize key content and prompt trainees to plan for actions they will need to take post-training.

☐ Dividing a training program into multiple sessions that offer a progressive series of projects or assignments to be accomplished between sessions.

☐ Time for practice activities within the training session.

☐ Time for clarification and discussion during the program.

☐ Modeling the instructor's behaviors during the training.

☐ Post-program assignments and goal setting.

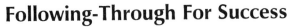
Following-Through For Success

Once you've planned for follow-through, and included it in your training, you're ready to work on it after the sessions have ended. Managers, the training staff, and the trainees themselves can all work on making training results last.

The manager's responsibilities

If you are a manager . . .

☑ **Provide an application assignment immediately following the program.**

☑ **Communicate the follow-through plan. Monitor and measure progress.**

☑ **Implement an action plan to identify and reduce workplace barriers that make it difficult to adopt newly learned behaviors.**

☑ **Reinforce improved performance and change.**

As a manager, you have to take an active role in the follow-through process. Provide opportunities for your employees to show off their new skills, talk about the changes, make it easy for them to change, and reward them for doing well.

The training staff's responsibilities

If you are a part of the training staff, you have a responsibility to support the manager's and trainees' follow-through efforts. You should:

☑ **Be available and offer support.**

☑ **Assist with data collection.**

☑ **Observe results, and recognize good efforts on everyone's part.**

☑ **Complete a thorough course evaluation.**

Training specialists shouldn't disappear when the course is complete. In fact, being available reveals a true commitment to training. Help in every way possible, especially with the evaluation, and be quick to commend those who are doing well. It's a good motivator!

The trainees' responsibilities

The initial period of practicing new behaviors and applying new skills is often awkward and uncertain. That is why support from managers and the training staff is vital to follow-through. But trainees can also speed up the process of learning. As a trainee who has just completed training, you should:

☑ **Ask for feedback from your manager and peers.**

☑ **Communicate ongoing needs to the training staff and your manager.**

Trainees do not need to wait for feedback from others. The faster it is requested and given, and the more specific it is, the faster the trainee will demonstrate good results. Likewise, constant communication about needs is essential to the success of any training effort. Management can only address needs if they know they are present.

Rachael stayed at Smithton Hotel . . .

to support the training effort and to ensure that the measurements were tabulated. The personal action plan the team designed as a checklist for the personnel really helped the training follow-through by providing a visual reminder of the skills taught during training.

In addition, supervisors were now instructed to check each room for adherence to the new cleanliness standards and procedures. And the incentive program, revised to include adherence to these new procedures, reinforced the newly learned skills. Six months down the line, the Housekeeping Department reached its goal of improving the customer comment cards and the Customer Satisfaction Index.

They were committed to follow-through—and it showed!

Most organizations spend considerable time and money on the presentation of training information, and give little attention to practice or implementation. The same situation plays itself out daily in the weight-loss business. Individuals spend billions of dollars to lose weight, only to gain the weight back after the program is finished. It's the follow-through that takes the success of a training effort and maintains it.

CHAPTER NINE WORKSHEET:
ENSURING FOLLOW-THROUGH

1. If you've yet to implement your training, list three things you or your staff can do to prepare for successful follow-through.

_____

_____

_____

_____

_____

_____

2. Describe two types of training activities that would help ensure that needs for training follow-through have been taken into account.

_____

_____

_____

_____

_____

3. Think about a recent training session or one that's upcoming. Design a simple checklist to measure improvement in skills or behavior that were or will be taught.

_____

_____

_____

_____

_____

_____

_____

_____

_____

_____

_____

_____

_____

_____

_____

_____

_____

CHAPTER TEN

SUMMARY

"No great man ever complains
of want of opportunity."

-Emerson

With the six phases of the High-IMPACT Training™ Model behind you, the complete picture of training should be in focus. The puzzle is finished, with no pieces missing.

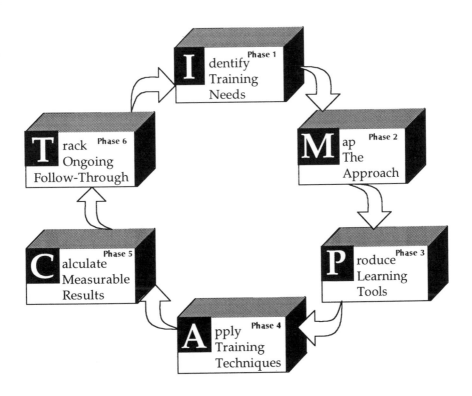

PHASE	DESCRIPTION
1. **I** dentify **Training Needs**	First, you **Identified** your training needs. You checked to see if training was actually needed and established what kind of role it would play in improving job performance.
2. **M** ap The **Approach**	Second, you **Mapped** your training approach. You settled on the training objectives that would take you to your goal. Then you analyzed your trainees so that you could design the best training approach for them.
3. **P** roduce **Learning Tools**	Third, you **Produced** effective learning tools. You chose the tools that would maximize the learning process, and then tailored them to fit your particular trainees and situation.
4. **A** pply Training **Techniques**	Fourth, you **Applied** successful training techniques. You utilized verbal and nonverbal delivery skills to increase your performing ability. You competently used the effective learning tools you produced in the previous phase. And you skillfully fielded questions.
5. **C** alculate **Measurable Results**	Fifth, you **Calculated** measurable training results. You evaluated participant response, both *"to"* and *"from"* the program. You assessed on-the-job action, analyzed business-driven results, and even tabulated the impact that the training had on your organization.
6. **T** rack Ongoing **Follow-Through**	Sixth, and finally, you **Tracked** training for lasting impact. You planned and provided for follow-through, ensuring that the effort you put into your training would pay off long after the sessions ended.

Whew! Training isn't a simple task. But when you know how to fit all the pieces of the puzzle together, you begin to see the beauty of the whole picture. Take the time and make the effort to create High-IMPACT training. You'll be rewarded with the satisfaction of improving job performance and increasing the success of your organization. You can't beat that claim!

REFERENCES AND REPRODUCIBLE FORMS

The pages in the Appendix are provided for you to photocopy and use appropriately.

ADVANTAGES AND DISADVANTAGES OF COMMON LEARNING METHODS

When designing training materials, more than likely you will be concerned with *"What is the most effective method for getting the content across to participants?"* Although there are no simple answers, it is important to consider the advantages and disadvantages for each of the most common learning methods.

TECHNIQUE/DESCRIPTION	ADVANTAGES	DISADVANTAGES
Lecture Delivery of content by the trainer	Information is concentrated and organized as desired Saves time	Relative passiveness of participants Depends totally on trainer's effectiveness and information
Structured Discussion Structured conversations between participants *(in small or large groups),* aimed toward specific learning objectives	Participant interaction and idea sharing Past experiences of participants contribute to the learning process	May be dominated by a few participants Potential creation of side discussions which don't apply

TECHNIQUE/DESCRIPTION	ADVANTAGES	DISADVANTAGES
Panel Discussion Short lectures or discussion by a variety of trainers *(or guests)*, rather than a single trainer	Offers a variety of viewpoints and delivery styles Helps stimulate different participant interests	Reduces participant responsibility since content is typically with the panelists May result in side debates which impacts planned timeframe
Reading Individual reading of participant materials during a structured timeframe	Expose participants to large quantities of content in a concentrated timeframe Opportunity to review materials during the course of reading	May seem tedious or boring to participants Difficult to hold participants accountable for content
Personal Action Planning Identifying specific activities that the participant is committing to carry out	Application of skills, knowledge, or behaviors back on the job Facilitates the documentation of key learnings while still in the classroom	Some participants may be unwilling to make a commitment to apply training Lack of specific follow-up and accountability

TRAINEE DEMOGRAPHICS MATRIX

Organization/Division: _____

Training Program: _____

Trainee Group	Demographics					
	Education	Math Skills	Language Skills	Age	Motivation	Historical Data

LEARNING METHODS CHECKLIST

Do I have . . .	1-On-1 Training	Small Group Training	Class-room Training	Self-Instructed Training	Video-tapes	CBT	Job-aids	Etc.
1. Adequate development time?								
2. Adequate program budget?								
3. Adequate resources: equipment and materials for development?								
4. Adequate staff and skills for this type of program?								
5. Appropriate learning environment and equipment?								
6. Appropriate instructional design (given audience and targeted learning domains)?								
7. Ease of update with this medium?								
8. Opportunities for repeated use?								
9. Opportunities for integration with other programs?								
10. Will this medium work in our output-driven culture?								
TOTALS								

PROGRAM MATERIAL CHECKLIST

Do I have . . .	Flip Charts	Over- heads	Slides	Printed Materials	Video- tapes	Computer Projection	Model	Etc.
1. Adequate development time?								
2. Adequate program budget?								
3. Adequate resources: equipment and materials for development?								
4. Adequate staff and skills for this type of program?								
5. Appropriate learning environment and equipment?								
6. Appropriate instructional design (given audience and targeted learning domains)?								
7. Ease of update with this medium?								
8. Opportunities for repeated use?								
9. Opportunities for integration with other programs?								
10. Will this medium work in our output-driven culture?								
TOTALS								

STORYBOARD PLANNING GUIDE

Program Title: _____   Page _____ of _____

	Key Points	Layout

Title: _____   _____

_____   _____

_____

Type: _____   _____

_____

Title: _____   _____

_____   _____

_____

Type: _____   _____

_____

Title: _____   _____

_____   _____

_____

Type: _____   _____

_____

Title: _____   _____

_____   _____

_____

Type: _____   _____

_____

Title: _____   _____

_____   _____

_____

Type: _____   _____

_____

TRAINER FEEDBACK AND EVALUATION

How well did the trainer . . .

		Poor	Fair	Good	Outstanding
1.	Show content mastery/knowledge of material? Comments:	1	2	3	4
2.	Walk through on-line functions, explain material, give instructions? Comments:	1	2	3	4
3.	Use examples/analogies to enhance learning and maintain interest? Comments:	1	2	3	4
4.	Use time effectively (*e.g. show organization, transition appropriately, prioritize tasks, etc.)*? Comments:	1	2	3	4
5.	Question participants to stimulate discussion and verify learning? Comments:	1	2	3	4
6.	Motivate participants (*i.e., show enthusiasm, encourage participation, demonstrate respect, etc.)*? Comments:	1	2	3	4
7.	Use vocal variety, volume, pace, and clarity? Comments:	1	2	3	4
8.	Use gestures, body movement, and eye contact? Comments:	1	2	3	4
9.	Use overheads, transparencies, and flipcharts? Comments:	1	2	3	4
10.	Overall rating of trainer Comments:	1	2	3	4

ADDITIONAL RESOURCES
FROM RICHARD CHANG ASSOCIATES, INC.
PUBLICATIONS DIVISION

Available through Richard Chang Associates, Inc. and training and organizational development resource catalogs worldwide.

PRACTICAL GUIDEBOOK COLLECTION

QUALITY IMPROVEMENT SERIES

Continuous Process Improvement

Continuous Improvement Tools Volume 1

Continuous Improvement Tools Volume 2

Step-By-Step Problem Solving

Meetings That Work!

Improving Through Benchmarking

Succeeding As A Self-Managed Team

Satisfying Internal Customers First!

Process Reengineering In Action

Measuring Organizational Improvement Impact

MANAGEMENT SKILLS SERIES

Coaching Through Effective Feedback

Expanding Leadership Impact

Mastering Change Management

On-The-Job Orientation And Training

Re-Creating Teams During Transitions

Planning Successful Employee Performance

Coaching For Peak Employee Performance

Evaluating Employee Performance

Interviewing And Selecting High Performers

HIGH-IMPACT TRAINING SERIES

Creating High-Impact Training

Identifying Targeted Training Needs

Mapping A Winning Training Approach

Producing High-Impact Learning Tools

Applying Successful Training Techniques

Measuring The Impact Of Training

Make Your Training Results Last

WORKPLACE DIVERSITY SERIES

Capitalizing On Workplace Diversity

Successful Staffing In A Diverse Workplace

Team Building For Diverse Work Groups

Communicating In A Diverse Workplace

Tools For Valuing Diversity

HIGH PERFORMANCE TEAM SERIES

Success Through Teamwork

Building A Dynamic Team

Measuring Team Performance

Team Decision-Making Techniques

Guidebooks are also available in fine bookstores.

Additional Resources
From Richard Chang Associates, Inc.
Publications Division

Personal Growth And Development Collection

Managing Your Career in a Changing Workplace

Unlocking Your Career Potential

Marketing Yourself and Your Career

Making Career Transitions

101 Stupid Things Series

101 Stupid Things Trainers Do To Sabotage Success

101 Stupid Things Supervisors Do To Sabotage Success

101 Stupid Things Salespeople Do To Sabotage Success

Training Products

Step-By-Step Problem Solving TooLKIT™

Meetings That Work! Practical Guidebook TooLPAK™

Continuous Improvement Tools Volume 1 Practical Guidebook TooLPAK™

Packaged Training Programs

High Involvement Teamwork™

Continuous Process Improvement

Videotapes

Mastering Change Management**

Quality: You Don't Have To Be Sick To Get Better*

Achieving Results Through Quality Improvement*

Total Quality: Myths, Methods, Or Miracles**
  Featuring Drs. Ken Blanchard and Richard Chang

Empowering The Quality Effort**
  Featuring Drs. Ken Blanchard and Richard Chang

Total Quality Video Series And Workbooks

Building Commitment**

Teaming Up**

Applied Problem Solving**

Self-Directed Evaluation**

* Produced by American Media Inc.   ** Produced by Double Vision Studios

EVALUATION AND FEEDBACK FORM

We need your help to continuously improve the quality of the resources provided through the Richard Chang Associates, Inc., Publications Division. We would greatly appreciate your input and suggestions regarding this particular guidebook, as well as future guidebook interests.

Please photocopy this form before completing it, since other readers may use this guidebook. Thank you in advance for your feedback.

Guidebook Title: _____

1. Overall, how would you rate your *level of satisfaction* with this guidebook? Please circle your response.

    Extremely Dissatisfied   Satisfied   Extremely Satisfied

         1   2   3   4   5

2. What specific *concepts or methods* did you find <u>most</u> helpful?

    _____
    _____

3. What specific *concepts or methods* did you find <u>least</u> helpful?

    _____
    _____

4. As an individual who may purchase additional guidebooks in the future, what *characteristics/features/benefits* are most important to you in making a decision to purchase a guidebook *(or another similar book)*?

    _____
    _____

5. What additional *subject matter/topic areas* would you like to see addressed in future guidebooks?

    _____
    _____

Name *(optional)*:_____

Address: _____

C/S/Z: _____   **Phone (   )** _____

PLEASE FAX YOUR RESPONSES TO: (714) 756-0853
OR CALL US AT: 1-800-756-8096